Stick to the Music

Stick to the Music

Scores of Orchestral Tales

collected by
John Boyden

Illustrations by Merrily Harpur

SOUVENIR PRESS

Contents

Introduction 7

The Best of British

    Beecham – in a Class of His Own 13

    Boult – Champion of English Music 29

    Barbirolli – Glorious John 39

    The Best of the Rest 46

A Little Trouble with the Language 57

The Maestros

    Toscanini – A Towering Inferno 67

    Klemperer – The Indomitable 73

    Eccentrics and Geniuses 85

Show-biz and Opera Houses 98

The Trials of Composers 107

The Orchestra Strikes Back 115

Last Word 126

INTRODUCTION

I grew up in an atmosphere of music and conductors. I went to my first concert when I was eight. I can remember gripping the railing, high up on the precipitous inside of the Royal Albert Hall, and looking down past my young fists at the brilliantly lit orchestra below.

Beecham was conducting the Royal Philharmonic Orchestra and my father was down there, playing the trumpet. The next four or five years were filled with Beecham stories. He became my hero, a charismatic personality who ignored normal, bourgeois standards of behaviour. In my young eyes he sparkled.

Then my father left the Royal Philharmonic for the London Philharmonic. Another new boy in the LPO at that time was Sir Adrian Boult. With gaining maturity my allegiance shifted from Beecham to Boult for, where the capriciousness of Beecham had seemed so raffish, so exciting, Boult's grand symphonic analysis introduced a logic and a majesty far more rewarding than mere entertainment.

As I watched the members of the orchestra produce the goods and the conductor wave his little stick (always tuned to a secure C major), I wondered how conductors had assumed such dominance in music. Their role has neither long nor particularly deep roots.

I was aware of the growing need throughout the nineteenth century and beyond for someone to hold together ever larger orchestras and choruses for the sake of unity, but I believed a simpler and less obvious cause lay behind their success.

Orchestras are now too large for audiences to register them as anything other than a faceless group of black suits clutching instruments. In order to humanise such a generalised organisation, a miracle ingredient is needed. A single figure is required to represent the anonymous players and to provide a focal point. That person is the conductor.

To an audience he is the fount of all wisdom. In the eyes of the orchestra he is often little more than an obstacle to their true fulfilment. Conductors are not always memorable. The famous oboist Alec Whittaker, when asked who had been conducting the previous evening, replied, 'Dunno – didn't look.'

A player I know in the London Symphony Orchestra attributes the success of a concert to the coming together of a series of random factors – the music being played, the temperature of the hall, the humidity, the sense of well-being of the orchestra, the receptiveness of the audience, and that rare piece of magic which, even he admits, defies definition. One certainty in his mind, however, is that it has precious little to do with the chap on the box.

Such an approach is unjust for, while being willing to condemn poor conductors for dragging orchestras down, he is not prepared to attribute successful performances to the influence of inspired ones. Orchestral musicians, when asked their opinions of a conductor, often reply, 'Duff— but at least he didn't get in the way.'

The truth is that conductors and their orchestras can develop attachments resulting from bonds of mutual contempt and hostility every bit as productive as those born of affection and admiration.

But the marketplace has difficulty coping with more than a certain number of geniuses. When one dies, another shuffles along to replace him. As Horenstein once said, it is like walking the plank. When one steps off the end, another takes his place.

The greatest conductor, at any given moment, is the one who has managed to snatch the baton of unquestioned authority from the most recently departed. A maestro who has been discounted for years may, at the death of another, miraculously acquire great interpretative insights and find himself lionised by the critics everywhere.

Conducting is about relationships. It concerns leadership. It is based upon the management of a group of individuals willing (for whatever motives) temporarily to submerge some of their idiosyncrasies for the good of the whole. In many ways orchestras and their conductors serve as some sort of lesson to the rest of us.

THE
BEST OF BRITISH

Beecham:
In a Class of His Own

Sir Thomas Beecham was born in 1879, the same year as Sir Hamilton Harty, and in many ways they had similar personalities. They shared a passion for Berlioz and an ability to revive neglected works of Handel, and both were lionised by their orchestra and audiences.

Beecham had recommended Harty's appointment to the Hallé in 1923 and had even directed the accompaniment to the composer's performance of his own piano concerto in the same year. Harty became in institution in Manchester, just as Sir John Barbirolli was to be in later years. Beecham, however, usually managed to steal Harty's thunder. He was determined to be top dog. Harty had no chance to recommend Beecham for any appointment – the latter never waited for organisations to offer him jobs but formed orchestras and opera companies in his own image with apparent ease.

Beecham's efforts to monopolise opera were not universally appreciated, not even by those who owed their jobs to him. Harty once observed, 'British opera is dying slowly but surely – of TB.'

But the final insult for Beecham, a Lancastrian

by birth, must have come when he demanded his usual suite at the Midland Hotel, Manchester.

'It's not available,' the girl told him.

'Do you know who I am? I am Sir Thomas Beecham and I intend to have the apartment.'

'I don't care if you're Sir Hamilton Harty – you can't have it this time.'

♪

While still a young man, and before fame overtook him, Beecham was once travelling in the first-class non-smoking compartment of a train.

No sooner had the train begun to move than an expensively dressed lady entered, smoking a cigarette. She took the seat immediately opposite him.

He stared at her with hostility until she could stand it no longer.

'I hope you don't mind my smoking like this?' she asked.

'Not at all, madam,' Beecham replied, 'but I trust that you won't mind too much when I am sick.'

The lady looked astonished. 'I don't think you can have any idea who I am. I am one of the directors' wives.'

'Really?' said Beecham. 'I don't care if you're the director's only wife. I shall still be sick.'

♩

Beecham's ability to harness an orchestra in pursuit of his own aims was exemplified by one occasion when he was conducting the Russian Ballet at Covent Garden. Anyone was fair game in his book, so long as his players were on his side. In a way he needed the adulation of two audiences – his own orchestra's and the paying public's.

During a rehearsal, one of the leading Russian male dancers approached the front of the stage, his leotards bursting with whip-like muscles, his feet splayed at that curious angle favoured by classical dancers and Charlie Chaplin.

He stared down at Beecham, who lolled on a stool in front of the orchestra.

'This,' the dancer declared, 'it is too slow. Too slow. We cannot dance like this. Too slow.'

'Don't worry,' Beecham replied. 'I'll pep it up a bit tonight.'

That evening, when the particular scene arrived, Beecham took the music at such a lick that the dancers found themselves dashing back and forth across the stage desperately trying to stay with the conductor's vigorous beat.

The scene finished, and the drained dancers were left, chests heaving, like so many landed trout on a river bank, clutching for support at the scenery and each other. Beecham turned his eyes left, then right, to his players along the pit.

'That made the beggars hop,' he smirked.

♩

Between the two world wars one of the most highly regarded concert pianists was the Austrian Artur Schnabel. His reputation rested on his interpretation of the great Viennese classics.

Schnabel was notorious for taking over rehearsals from the conductor. He had a habit of instructing individual players in the orchestra without the least regard for the conductor's standing.

At the end of a concert with the London Philharmonic during the 1930s, Sir Thomas Beecham asked Frank Probyn, a horn player, who was due to play the concerto next day. When Probyn told him it was Schnabel, Beecham looked thoughtful.

The following morning the rehearsal hall was alive with noisy bustle. At ten o'clock the players took their places. The revered figure of Schnabel was already at the keyboard, ready to get to work. But where was Beecham?

Five, then ten, minutes elapsed – still no Sir Thomas. After twenty minutes of finely judged absence, he arrived and marched briskly onto the rostrum entirely ignoring the soloist.

Beecham raised his arms. He pretended suddenly to notice Schnabel seated at one end of the nine-foot Steinway. He lowered his arms.

'Why are you here?' he asked as though surprised.

'To rehearse, of course,' Schnabel answered, astonished by the question.

'Not now, you can't,' Sir Thomas replied firmly. 'I've got more than one or two things to sort out before we get to you. Why don't you go and sit down over there?' He waved airily towards the seats in the hall. 'I'll give you a call when we're ready.'

The stunned pianist left the platform, meekly recognising the weakness of his position.

Sir Thomas set about rehearsing with a rare bad humour a symphony not even on that evening's programme, sniping at his excellent players. First, he took the horns apart.

'Much better in the Berlin Philharmonic,' he snapped.

The players knew him too well to take this show of bad temper seriously and soon began to play up to it. The wretched Schnabel was forced to witness this unhappy rehearsal and to wait his turn. Any thoughts he might have had of overriding this particular conductor evaporated in the face of such arrogance.

The break in the rehearsal passed, and still Beecham ignored his soloist. What should Schnabel do? How could he re-establish himself without appearing foolish? Then, with only thirty minutes of the rehearsal remaining, Sir Thomas turned to him.

'I'm ready for you now, Mr Schnabel,' he beamed. 'We've just time enough for a quick run-through.'

It is not widely appreciated how much Beecham relied on his players to give of their best, for his conducting technique was far from perfect. One of the most effective ways he found to encourage maximum cooperation was to avoid making jokes at the expense of players within the orchestra. His jests were turned against outsiders, so that his orchestra became a sort of closed community, displaying a unified front to the outside world.

During the 1930s the Leeds Festival enjoyed considerable eminence and the quality of the Festival Chorus was well established. They gave important concerts under the greatest names of the day. None was greater than Sir Thomas's, who took his newly formed London Philharmonic to play with the chorus.

One day, when rehearsing in Leeds Town Hall, he was nearing the end of an orchestral item while the members of the chorus were waiting their turn outside. Through the glass of the closed doors the assembled mass of singers could be seen jostling eagerly.

Beecham half turned towards the doors and nodded in the direction of some of the more elderly singers.

'Gentlemen,' he declared in his most pompous manner, 'waiting outside those doors are enough varicose veins to stretch from here to Brighton.'

♪

Gerald Jackson was one of the last great exponents of the wooden flute. He played for Beecham in the London Philharmonic before the war, and in the Royal Philharmonic Orchestra for the first eleven years of its existence. On one occasion during his time with the LPO he became fed up with the vagueness of Beecham's beat.

Throughout the entire first half of the concert he had been struggling to place his notes with precision and finally ran out of patience when the chords at the end of the slow movement of Brahms' Violin Concerto were reached.

'I've had enough of this,' he said to the principal oboe, 'it's got beyond a joke.'

'Don't go off the deep end at me,' exclaimed his colleague. 'If you feel so strongly about it, go and tell him yourself. Don't tell me.'

Jackson went in seach of Sir Thomas and found him in his room, feet up, with a cigar and a drink.

'Yes?' queried Sir Thomas when he saw Jackson in the doorway. 'What do you want?'

'I've had enough, Sir Thomas,' he began. 'It's all too damned nerve-racking out there trying to work out where your beat is.'

Sir Thomas puffed his cigar.

'And where was this?' he asked casually, taking another puff. 'Where was it that you had all this trouble?'

'The end of the slow movement, Sir Thomas,'

Jackson explained, surprised at Beecham's calmness.

'Well, was it in tune?'

'Yes, Sir Thomas.'

'Was it together?'

'Yes, Sir Thomas.'

'Was it in time?'

'Yes, Sir Thomas, it was.'

'Then what on earth are you complaining about?'

Sir Thomas took a sip of his drink and looked up from his chair. 'Close the door on your way out, there's a good chap.'

♩

Orchestral librarians have little glamour in their job but they nevertheless perform a vital function: mistakes can have unhappy consequences. They have, however, been known to put out the wrong music on the players' stands or to arrange it in the wrong sequence.

At the beginning of a concert outside London, Beecham suddenly found himself directing a sort of chaos. Half the Royal Philharmonic were playing one piece while the rest were happily playing another.

Sir Thomas flung his stick into his music stand, his face a mixture of confusion and disbelief. Clearly the librarian had got it wrong and nobody had bothered to check the parts.

The orchestra's cacophony staggered to a halt (some years ahead of the market for such stuff) and Sir Thomas turned to face his startled audience. He stroked his chin.

'There seems to be a slight discrepancy,' he mused with calculated irony, 'about what we should be playing for you.'

The audience stirred in their seats.

'What does it say in your programmes?' he asked, cupping a hand to his ear to hear more easily the shouted response. Several people called out the work's name.

'Well, in that case,' he declared, 'we'll play what you've got down there, and not what the other half of the gentlemen of the orchestra thought they should be playing – whatever that was.'

♩

On one occasion Beecham was to direct a concert performance of Handel's *Messiah*. His soprano was nervous of the piece: she had never sung it and she suffered from a stammer, but Sir Thomas told her to get on with it anyway.

They met the day before the concert and she proudly showed him the score.

'How's it going now?' he asked.

'I-I-I'll be all right t-t-tomorrow, Sir T-T-Thomas,' she said. 'I've been studying the music for weeks and I-I-I've been taking the score with

me everywhere. I-I-I've even been taking it up to
b-b-bed at night with me . . .'

'Then, in that case I'm sure we shall have an
immaculate conception.'

♩

Just after the war Beecham allowed himself to be
cajoled by the BBC into directing a studio-bound
performance of Berlioz's colossal and rarely
heard opera, *The Trojans*. He had no love for the
BBC, but allowed his resentment to be overcome
by some substantial fees for his newly formed
Royal Philharmonic Orchestra.

The leader of the orchestra was David McCallum. He was, or thought he was, fully accustomed to Sir Thomas's little jests. But, when the
end of the first act was reached and Beecham
continued to flail the air long after the music had
stopped, he must have begun to wonder.

McCallum was in a quandary over what to do.
Eventually, he looked up at Sir Thomas, still
busily beating time.

'The piece is over, Sir Thomas,' he called
gently.

Beecham put down his stick. 'And about time
too!' he said, and walked off.

♩

One of the disadvantages of our present concert

scene is the way in which the pressure of making box-office receipts balance costs has been relaxed. A combination of well-intentioned, yet often ill-conceived, government subsidies and the proliferation of alternative forms of entertainment has made it impossible for routine symphony concerts to pay their way.

Such changes have also wrought wonders on the mental approach of promoters and conductors, once the sole financers of orchestras. (From the orchestral players' point of view, one of Sir Thomas Beecham's most endearing features was the way he paid them.) The roles have been reversed: today it is the orchestras who employ the conductors.

Before the leading orchestras became as dependent on their annual fix from the Arts Council as any thin-faced junky, matters were somewhat different.

At one time in the late 1940s Sir Thomas was talked into mounting a concert in the Empress Hall, a vast exhibition centre not unlike Earls Court. A couple of days before the concert he was told that bookings were dreadful, with no more than three or four hundred people likely to turn out to hear the Royal Philharmonic in their great barn. The crafty knight, mindful of potential losses, worked out a plot to stave off disaster.

As soon as he walked into the hall for his first rehearsal, he took one look and announced, 'I'm not conducting in a place like this. You can't expect artists to work here. It's too cold.' He stalked out.

A well-placed mole soon leaked the story to Fleet Street. 'Sir Thomas walks out.' 'Will he do the concert?' ran the headlines.

Of course, Beecham had arranged for someone else to rehearse the orchestra in his absence. His scheme worked: several thousand people braved the weather to see if he would turn up and, if he did so, whether he would say something controversial.

Beecham directed the entire proceedings – he was not likely to miss a good house. Would any modern conductor think so positively, so constructively or, dare one say it, so commercially?

♪

During the 1950s Toscanini's brilliant young pupil, Guido Cantelli, flashed briefly across the musical heavens before his tragic death in an air crash in 1956. He was lauded by the press and given an impressive recording contract by EMI.

There was a certain poignancy attached to Cantelli's meeting with Sir Thomas Beecham, for the latter had some years earlier declined Walter Legge's offer of the principal conductorship of the Philharmonia.

Cantelli had been recording with the Philharmonia inside the Royal Festival Hall, and was leaving the building while Sir Thomas was arriving to give a concert with his own Royal Philharmonic Orchestra.

At that time the Royal Festival Hall was still incomplete and artists had no choice but to use the large and ponderous instrument lift to reach the concert platform three floors up.

Cantelli, accompanied by one of the Philharmonia's management, stood waiting as the huge green lift gates slid open, to reveal the unmistakable figure of Sir Thomas, together with that of a diminutive violinist who had been trying to avoid contact with Beecham on the way up by skulking at the opposite end of the lift.

'Sir Thomas,' declared the man from the Philharmonia with considerable pride, 'let me introduce to you the young Italian maestro, Guido Cantelli.'

Beecham looked frostily at his sleek, young rival.

'Delighted to meet you,' he declared and, advancing rapidly towards the humble fiddler, he took his hand with great warmth. 'I've heard so much about you.'

And was gone.

♪

There can have been few conductors as dissimilar in temperament as Sir Thomas Beecham and Sir Adrian Boult. The former was a roguish wit who delighted in shocking people and who rejected the idea of being a member of the establishment (it would be hard to think of Beecham directing the music for one Coronation, let alone two, as Boult did). The latter was a modest intellectual who saw his role as being that of a servant to the needs of the composer's score and the welfare of his many colleagues.

Beecham ate, smoked and drank more than was good for him and clearly enjoyed the acclaim of crowds and audiences throughout the world; Boult, however, was more than happy to stay in Britain. He was one of the last conductors to hiss into silence an audience intent on applauding in a cathedral. Nevertheless, it must be mentioned that Beecham, although not overtly a religious man, did summarily sack a leader of his orchestra who had propped his feet on the high altar in Canterbury Cathedral during a rehearsal!

Boult's sense of occasion was so sharp that he maintained that applause at the end of Brahms' or Elgar's Second Symphonies destroyed the sense of mystery, of inevitable decline into nothingness. He received an audience's adulation at the end of a concert more for the sake of the orchestra than to satisfy any emotional need of his own.

These two very different musical knights passed through life on very different routes and in search of very different goals. Boult was truthful – Beecham less so. Boult was a man of controlled passion. Beecham seemed to have little control.

One excelled in the German classics, the other veered heavily towards French culture.

Shortly before his death, early in 1961, Sir Thomas was visited at his house in St John's Wood by the music journalist Evan Senior.

Sir Thomas was propped up in bed with a large drink in his hand.

'Just been visited by Adrian,' he announced between sips. 'Worthy chap, Adrian. Very worthy. Splendid character. Positively reeks of Horlicks!'

Boult:
Champion of English Music

Ten years younger than Beecham, Sir Adrian Boult was the first conductor to work closely with the newly established British Broadcasting Corporation. He formed the BBC Symphony Orchestra and remained its conductor until his enforced retirement in 1950 (under BBC rules he was required to retire at the age of 60).

A few years later, still smarting at what he saw as a premature dismissal, he accepted an invitation to return as guest conductor. As he took his place on the rostrum in the main studio, he looked up at the electric clock high on the wall behind the orchestra. He noticed that the hands had stuck.

'Get the clock going,' he instructed, 'or I'll stop the rehearsal in ten minutes' time – when the clock says so.'

The management got into a frightful sweat and, fearful of Boult's threat, sent a man with a brown coat, who took the hands off altogether. Such is bureaucracy!

The hands were missing for a year.

Different backgrounds often produce very different ideas of what is important for success. This point is well illustrated by a meeting between Sir Adrian Boult and Sir John Barbirolli, both great Elgarians.

Sir Adrian's view of conducting was conditioned by an Edwardian detachment which held that the conductor's role was to assist an orchestra to achieve self-expression within a framework of respect for the composer's score.

Barbirolli, on the other hand, approached conducting with an insight into what actually took place on the shop floor – for in his younger days, in common with Toscanini, he had been a very fine cellist.

Some time after the Second World War, Sir Adrian invited Sir John to take the BBC Symphony Orchestra for a week's concerts. The following week they met over lunch.

'How did you find the orchestra?' asked Sir Adrian.

Sir John cleared his throat. 'You know that chap sitting at number three in the seconds?' he asked in his gravelly London voice.

'Certainly. What about him?'

'He's not very good, you know. You ought to get rid of him.'

'Get rid of him!' exclaimed a shocked Sir Adrian. 'What on earth do you mean? Get rid of him! Why, he's an Oxford man.'

The leader of the BBC Symphony Orchestra was retiring. This was to be his last appearance with the orchestra and, not surprisingly, he was feeling somewhat sad.

He was a great enthusiast for Elgar and was thrilled when he discovered that the main work in his final broadcast was to be the great A-flat Symphony.

Halfway through the recording of the first movement, which is full of powerful and turbulent ideas, he looked up at the figure of Sir Adrian Boult sweeping his way through the familiar and deeply loved pages.

The leader felt good. All was well with the world – Elgar on the stand and Boult on the box. Suddenly he realised that the conductor was bending down in his direction. What did he want? There was nothing wrong. The performance was going splendidly.

Through the splendour of the blazing brass and the strings' slashing drive, Boult put a question to him.

'It is beef on Thursdays, isn't it?'

The conductor continued to propel the music, his mind on his lunch.

'I'm not sure, Sir Adrian,' the leader replied.

Boult straightened his ramrod back and drove the orchestra headlong into the rest of the symphony's intricacies. Eight or nine minutes passed before he leaned down again.

'I think it is, you know,' he concluded with a smile, his great long stick describing swirling arcs in the air.

♩

The Scottish National Orchestra and Chorus were rehearsing under Boult in a large and resonant hall. For a couple of hours the conductor had stood shouting against an unrelenting echo, trying to make himself understood.

At one point he called for the choir to make an alteration to their music. They stared at him, not comprehending what was being said as his words were swallowed up in the vastness of the auditorium. Fortunately the leader of the orchestra, appreciating the breakdown in communications, told him that the choir had no pencils.

'Then they must bring pencils tomorrow,' he said.

Next day, soon after the start of the rehearsal, Sir Adrian asked the choir to alter their parts once more. But the choir were still without pencils.

'I told you to bring pencils yesterday,' he snapped. 'Where are they?'

'They couldn't have heard you properly, Sir Adrian,' the leader suggested, interceding on the singers' behalf.

The British knight was undeterred. 'I asked for pencils. They should have brought pencils.' Adding with finality, 'No pencils – no rehearsal.'

He marched off to his room and banged the door behind him.

Everybody on the platform sat still, nonplussed by his disappearance. After a while the orchestra deputed someone to go to bring their conductor back. The chorus and orchestra waited, fascinated to see what would happen next.

'Sir Adrian,' the messenger called as he tapped timidly on the heavy door.

'Go away,' ordered the angry conductor. 'No pencils – no rehearsal.'

'But, Sir Adrian,' the messenger went on, 'they simply didn't hear you, that's all. The hall's too resonant, it makes it very hard to understand what anyone's saying. They weren't being rude. They're all very sorry.'

'It's not enough. It's not professional,' Boult replied from behind the door. 'They should know better. What's the matter with them?'

The rejected messenger retreated to the stage.

Fortunately, attached to the Scottish National Orchestra was an old colleague of Sir Adrian from prewar days with the BBC Symphony Orchestra. He was sent for. This time, once he heard the familiar voice making excuses for everybody else's unprofessionalism, Sir Adrian allowed himself to be enticed from his bolt hole.

'I'm sorry,' he said, and everything was restored to normality.

♩

Although it is often argued that music is a universal culture, certain barriers to full appreciation do occur. Particular national styles refuse to cross frontiers, often for no explicable reason. Why has the music of Sibelius, for instance, never taken root in Germany?

Among our major composers it is Vaughan Williams whose music suffers the greatest rejection overseas. His grey-greenness, his mystical Englishness, offer few signposts to audiences more used to primary colours.

It is true that his piece *The Fen Country*, in common with the great tracts of flat land the work describes, is something of an acquired taste and offers little help to the unaccustomed ear. Doubtless the lack of understanding shown by alien listeners to this atmospheric piece can be explained by all sorts of complicated theories, but Sir Adrian Boult's was both simple and direct.

Sir Adrian was once recording it with the Philharmonia Orchestra, whose leader was a young violinist from South America, Carlos Villa. After a couple of takes, Boult asked Carlos what he thought of the piece.

'I don't like it, Sir Adrian,' he replied.

'Oh, really,' said the conductor.

Later, at the end of the session, Sir Adrian was being driven home together with the recording producer, and thought he should make polite conversation.

'Mr Villa doesn't like *The Fen Country*,' he said.

'Oh, really,' replied the producer, 'why not?'

'Well, he wouldn't, would he? He's a foreigner.'

♪

Boult rarely went to North America. On one of the few occasions when he did venture across the Atlantic, he was engaged by a prominent American orchestra.

Inevitably, because of his association with this century's renaissance of English music, the programme included works by Vaughan Williams and Elgar.

During the rehearsal everything went well. Boult eliminated some of the less couth qualities of the orchestra's approach and contrived to plaster on some of the expressive *nobilmente* for which he was so famous.

However, when it came to the concert, matters reverted to their previous state. The brass brayed, the strings swooped and the percussion took on an attack and brilliance which would not have been out of place in a fine marching band. Boult was not happy.

Annoyed, he took the leader, or concertmaster, to one side and demanded to know why they had turned in performances so utterly different from the rehearsal.

'Well, Sir Boult, you see, it's like this,' the leader began, as though explaining the obvious, 'the rehearsal's all yours – but the concert's all ours.'

One of the reasons why certain artists rise to the top of the pile is that they possess, apart from natural ability, an extraordinary capacity for taking pains, for pursuing relentlessly what seem to be unattainable and perhaps even irrelevant aims.

When the musician is alone, performing his own unique conceptions, few constraints are placed on him, but when giving a concerto he must make at least a gesture towards unity with the conductor and his orchestra.

Some years ago Moura Lympany – then, as now, our leading woman pianist – was touring overseas with the London Philharmonic under Sir Adrian Boult. Midway through one of the rehearsals she got herself into a muddle. Try as she might, she could not cajole the particular sound she wanted from the piano.

Sir Adrian stood loftily on the rostrum and the orchestra sat quietly while Miss Lympany struggled.

After a while Sir Adrian leaned over to ask what the problem might be. It sounded all right to him.

'I can't get it the way I want it,' she insisted, preparing for another attempt at the passage.

'Fortunately, my dear,' Boult replied, 'as no one has the least idea how you want it to sound, nobody's going to be any the wiser if you succeed. So there's little point in worrying about it, is there?'

♩

When already well into his nineties, Boult had to attend the Queen Mother to receive a diploma. His usual driver was unavailable to take him from his flat in West Hampstead (or Kilburn, as Boult preferred to call it), so he hired a car from an unfamiliar source.

Because his legs had given out, he was carried from his flat, in considerable discomfort, by the new chauffeur. On the way down to the car, they collided with a couple of doorposts before the old man was unceremoniously dumped in the Rolls.

When they reached Clarence House Sir Adrian decided that enough was enough and refused to leave the car. He might have lost the use of his legs but he still had his wits about him.

'It would be better for everyone were the documents to be brought out to me,' he declared.

The driver went into the house. He returned with an equerry, who told Sir Adrian that he would take care of everything.

Almost immediately a flunky appeared clutching a small awning, which he erected on four poles in the street to the side of the Rolls' rear door. He was followed by a couple of footmen with a small table and a golden chair.

The Queen Mother arrived, complete with diploma, followed by a footman with tea set out on a silver tray, which he placed on the table between the Queen Mother and Sir Adrian, who was still seated on the Rolls' back seat. They proceeded to have tea in the street.

Once the diploma had been handed over, the Queen Mother went back indoors. Along the street ambled a policeman. He came across to Sir Adrian.

'Do you realise, sir,' he asked in a properly pompous manner, 'that you are sitting in an unlicensed vehicle?'

Barbirolli:
Glorious John

Although his approach to music was very different from that of Toscanini, Sir John Barbirolli
worshipped the artistry of the great Italian conductor. Such adoration may have been due to a
bond of nationality, imagined or real (for Sir
John's parents were Italian and he was christened
Giovanni); or it may simply have been that he
recognised the genius of the older man.

Whatever it was, there can be no doubt that Sir
John's regard for Toscanini survived the extremely tough time which he was forced to
endure when, shortly before the war, he followed him as principal conductor of the New
York Philharmonic.

One of Toscanini's more obvious habits was to
move onto the platform at the outset of a concert
with his right arm bent up behind his back.

Soon after Toscanini's death, Barbirolli gave a
concert in the Royal Festival Hall to which Sir
Adrian Boult had been invited. The orchestra had
taken their places and completed their tuning,
when from the curtained doorway to the left of
the stage emerged the small and stooping figure
of Sir John. But what was this? Where was the
right arm which had formerly swung so free?
Why was it bent up behind his back?

'Ah,' said Sir Adrian, with a knowing smile, 'the Maestro.'

♩

Barbirolli was on a tour of South America and was sitting with a group of players in an airport waiting-room, bored by the interminable schedule of travel and concerts. He pulled back his sleeve.

'Look at this watch,' he said.

They all looked hard at the splendid gold wristwatch.

'I got it for being rude to Heifetz,' he announced with a straight face.

The musicians looked astonished at such a suggestion.

'Before the war, when I was with the New York Philharmonic, I was conducting in the Hollywood Bowl. Heifetz was the soloist in the Tchaikovsky concerto. When we got to the oboe solo which the soloist follows he spoke directly to the player – he paid no attention to me. I might as well not have been there. "Not like that," he said, "do it like this."

'I wasn't having that, so I said, "He'll do it the way I want him to do it." So Heifetz walked off the platform. Someone in the orchestra must have told Horowitz. Anyway, when Horowitz heard about it he sent me this watch. Good, isn't it?'

♩

Sir John took a keen interest in the personal welfare of everyone in his orchestra, the Hallé. He knew that the very best performances require every player to be, at worst, contented or, at best, happy.

Only cricket and possibly food and drink came anywhere near competing with his passion for music. He could not begin to understand anyone allowing any interference with his art.

One day the wife of one of the Hallé players came to him. She was in a dreadful state, weighed down with concern and close to tears. Between sobs and great gulps for air she managed haltingly to tell Sir John the reason for her misery. Slowly he realised that the lady's husband, now in early middle age, had slipped the halter and formed an alliance with a younger woman.

'What shall I do?' she wailed, twisting a sodden handkerchief between her whitened knuckles. 'He's all I've got.'

Sir John tried to pacify her and offered her a drink. She declined. He tried to take her hands but they writhed in her lap like well-meshed gears.

'What shall I do?' she repeated, staring wildly into his eyes for an answer.

'Well, my dear. There's really nothing to worry about,' Sir John began soothingly.

'Things are not all that bad, you know. After all, he is playing better than ever.'

Every week during the season, the bass section of the Hallé Orchestra formed a syndicate to enter the football pools. One day they were grouped in deep debate, away from the prying eyes of the rest of the orchestra, when Sir John Barbirolli passed by.

'What are you up to?' he asked.

'We're doing the pools, Sir John,' they said.

'Do you know, I've never done the pools. Can I have a go?'

'Of course,' they said.

'What do I have to do?' he asked.

'Just put some crosses in these little boxes here,' one of the bass players advised.

Later that week, when they checked their entry, they found that Sir John's line had won them £800. They agreed to tell him of their success – which, after all, had been entirely due to his impromptu skill in choosing numbers. It also seemed appropriate to give him a present of some kind, so they searched out the biggest bottle of scotch in Manchester.

'Do you think it'll be all right for us to go up and see him now?' they asked the Hallé's manager.

'Of course,' he agreed, 'he'll love it. I'll come along with you and we can tell him all about it.'

So the syndicate and the manager made their way up the stairs at the back of the Free Trade Hall and squeezed into the conductor's small room. The principal bass player held the huge bottle in front of him.

'Well, I'll be blowed,' Sir John said once they had told him of his skill, 'and what have you got there?'

'The biggest bottle of scotch we could find,' the principal replied.

'Good,' said the musical knight, turning to the Hallé's manager. 'This calls for a celebration, don't you think so, Wally?' He paused for thought. 'Fetch two glasses.'

♩

Barbirolli had taken the Hallé Orchestra on a tour which included Dubrovnik. Summer in Dubrovnik has a distinct edge over Manchester and while visiting the cathedral he was overcome by the heat and the humidity. He decided to rest a while on the steps.

Taking off his large broad-brimmed black hat,

he threw it to the ground alongside his abandoned cane. At the same time, he closed his eyes behind dark glasses. Soon he fell asleep.

When he awoke he found that passing supplicants on their way to mass, convinced that this sad figure must be in dire need of charity, had tossed the equivalent of £3.50 into his hat.

Unabashed, Sir John displayed this windfall to the orchestra before that evening's concert and explained, at some length, the ease with which an entirely new career had been opened to him.

♩

Barbirolli was justifiably proud of the Gold Medal of the Sibelius Society which he had received in Helsinki shortly before making a tour of the Caribbean with the Philharmonia Orchestra.

Throughout the flight from London and the many shorter flights and coach journeys between engagements, he fingered the gold medal and showed it proudly to the orchestra's leader, and to anyone else who happened by.

'Look at this!' he would say. 'Got it for what I did for the old boy's music!'

Certainly it is true that Sir John had given many fine performances of Sibelius's symphonies and tone poems over the years, particularly with his own Hallé Orchestra, and that he felt completely at home with the bleak northern idiom of the great Finn's powerful conceptions.

However, at one point on the tour, as the orchestra trooped down the steps of a plane to a welcoming committee, they were greeted by the rhythmic sounds of a local steel band. Sir John made a great flourish with his large black Verdi hat in the direction of the colourful musicians.

Together with all the members of the orchestra, he stood listening intently and applauded the performance when it finished with generous enthusiasm. Then he walked slowly towards the airport terminal, arm in arm with the leader.

'What was that piece they were playing?' he asked.

'Finlandia,' came the answer.

The Best
of the Rest

The great Sir Henry Wood took endless pains to get things right. It is nearly impossible for us to imagine what musical life in London was like a hundred years ago, before the benefit of his influence, when one of the best orchestras was that of the Royal Artillery.

Sir Henry dragged public taste out of the smoke of the music hall and into the airy light of the Promenade Concerts. He offered his audiences old favourites mixed with new sounds and new names, and, through a combination of window dressing and genuine hard work, he succeeded more than anyone in improving musical taste in this country.

Because he had only one rehearsal for each concert (and he conducted six a week for the eight-week season), he could afford to take no chances. In common with many a military bandmaster, he checked the tuning of each instrument before each concert.

The sound of his voice saying, 'A little up. A little down,' lived in many musicians' memories long after he had retired. What he failed to realise was that, on many occasions, the crafty players would send the same instrument through for inspection several times.

♪

Sir Henry was a natural Londoner. He did not speak with the tones of Eton and Oxford. He had no polished manner (neither did Beethoven), but he did go to the heart of a piece of music with rare intensity.

He had a habit of addressing the players with hanging prepositions: 'What are you cellos doing, regardless of?' Or: 'What are you trombones a-doing of?'

One of his friends took him to one side. 'Look. Henry, you oughtn't to have hanging prepositions like that at the end of sentences. It sounds rather bad.'

At the next rehearsal Sir Henry remembered this advice.

'What do you violins think you're doing?' he asked.

There was a pause, followed by the whole orchestra shouting with one voice, 'Regardless of!'

♪

Sir Hamilton Harty, now largely forgotten, was a wonderful conductor. His Berlioz was especially marvellous. Unlike Beecham and Toscanini, who both sang their music examples out of tune, Harty whistled his – in tune.

He also had a ready line of wit. He was once

instructing a trumpet player to play softer. 'Go on, softer still,' he urged.

'But, Sir Hamilton, it's marked *forte*.'

'Well, make it twenty.'

But the most charming story about Harty concerns a concert he gave with the ubiquitous Schnabel. They were in the middle of Brahms' Second Piano Concerto, when Schnabel had a lapse of memory.

Quick as a flash Harty realised the error and held up two fingers of one hand, making a throat-cutting motion with the other. The Hallé, as one man, skipped two bars and the performance continued with no one else the wiser. A tremendous achievement.

After the concert, Schnabel somewhat complacently said to Sir Hamilton, 'You know, the Hallé is nearly as good as the Berlin Philharmonic.'

'They're better,' Sir Hamilton replied, with good reason, 'two bars better.'

♪

During the Second World War conditions for symphony orchestras in Britain were appalling – particularly for the London Philharmonic, which only stayed in business through a combination of self-help and support from such unlikely sources as Jack Hylton, the dance-band leader.

At the blackest point of the war they were

engaged for a concert in the north of England. The orchestra's drivers went to collect the instrument van from a lock-up garage. Standing outside were a couple of policemen.

'You can't go in there,' they said. 'A bomb's dropped inside. You'll have to wait till the disposal people turn up – and God knows when that'll be.'

The undaunted drivers found another van and a duplicate set of instruments. Later that day, loaded down with music and instruments, they drove north through the bitter gloom of wartime winter.

When they reached the hall they set out the stands and instruments on the platform for the orchestra, who knew nothing of this drama.

The conductor, Basil Cameron, was a quiet man who often mumbled when addressing the orchestra. In fact, he must have been aware of this defect for occasionally and at random he would cup his hands together to form the cone of a megaphone and project his voice with greater impact to the back of the orchestra.

Not surprisingly, on this evening the librarian had been unable to find alternative copies of the music originally advertised, so Cameron was asked to explain to the audience the reason for the changes.

He began a typically long-winded explanation of the events in London and why the programme had necessarily been so altered. He mumbled away until, as was his habit, he cupped his hands to his mouth and announced quite sharply, 'Time bomb.'

The audience, not having registered the earlier part of his garbled message, fled from the hall in near panic. Soon the place was deserted. The entire London Philharmonic Orchestra gazed helplessly at rows of empty seats. They had driven hundreds of miles and left without playing a single note.

♩

A brilliant 'double-octave' pianist, of international standing, was engaged to play the Schumann Concerto for a routine Sunday evening concert in the Royal Albert Hall. The orchestra was there, the conductor, George Weldon, was ready to run through the concerto. It was nearly eleven in the morning, and time for the arrival of the pianist.

Finally the soloist appeared from the back of the platform, and fairly danced through the orchestra to his shiny black instrument at the front of the stage. The conductor smiled at him. Ready?

'I don't want to play the Schumann today,' announced the soloist, 'but I'll play the Grieg.'

Weldon looked surprised, the orchestra looked amused, the librarian looked shocked. But the soloist was adamant. So the parts for the Grieg were found and the rehearsal got under way again.

At the end, when all the musicians were beating their hasty paths to their cars outside the hall, the conductor and the leader both strolled over to the soloist.

'I'd love to know,' Weldon said, 'why you wouldn't do the Schumann. I've heard you play it lots of times, and you do it really well.'

'You're very kind,' the pianist replied, 'but the reason's not really very interesting.'

The leader was even more inquisitive than Weldon. 'I'm sure we'd both like to hear it,' he said.

'Well, it was like this. Last week I played the Schumann in Prague,' he hesitated slightly, 'and the conductor fell dead into the piano!'

'Good heavens!' exclaimed Weldon, 'what an awful thing.'

'Exactly,' the pianist agreed. And as he went through the motions of playing double octaves, he reached the nub of his explanation. 'You see, once he fell across the strings – I couldn't get any tone!'

♪

During the 1970s medieval music began to enjoy a revival of popularity. No one did more to achieve this breakthrough in public taste than the late David Munrow. At one time he was involved with several similar early-music ensembles, and while it would be difficult to describe anyone as being a 'conductor' of such music, he

nonetheless had an influence far beyond that of a mere member of the group.

At a particular concert, the members of one of these ensembles were presented to the Queen Mother. As is the custom, they were drawn up in a long line, each player holding his appropriate instrument. All sorts were on display, from rebecs, to crumhorns and recorders to nakers (pronounced nackers).

The nakers are small timpani, or kettledrums, brought from the Middle East by the crusaders. They are small copper bowls covered with taut skin and struck with short wooden sticks, and are held to the waist by a leather thong which leaves the player free to walk or dance while performing.

As the Queen Mother moved along the line, she stopped and said a few words to each performer, asking pertinent questions and generally being as interested in an obscure subject as could be expected.

The player of those dangerous instruments, the nakers, was a well-known and somewhat eccentric academic capable of considerable indiscretion. It is easy to imagine Munrow's worry when he began to appreciate the potential for embarrassment that lay in wait at the end of the line of musicians.

The Queen Mother continued her progress until at last she arrived at the nakers. She flicked their skins with a forefinger and walked on, only observing as she passed, 'They're a fine little pair.'

♩

One of the glories of British orchestras has always been the quality of the wind playing. Perhaps it is the natural individuality of our people that makes them prefer to play instruments with independent parts – rather than strings, which tend to play *en masse*.

One very well-known oboe player, and a great individualist, was Alec Whittaker. He was principal in the Philharmonia Orchestra during some of its greatest days, when they spent most of their time in the recording studio under conductors such as Furtwängler, Von Karajan and Cantelli, rarely venturing outside to give concerts.

At that time the corporate spirit of the orchestra, the belief that they were head and shoulders above the rest of their contemporaries, was total. After all, one of their guest conductors had been the almighty Toscanini.

During those halcyon days they were blessed with the presence on the rostrum of Sir Malcolm Sargent. It can be assumed without too much fear of contradiction that the Philharmonia would not have been in awe of the darling of the Promenaders. As one particular rehearsal got under way:

'Oboe,' called out Sir Malcolm in his snappy way, 'oboe. You are flat.'

Whittaker stared with unfocused eyes.

'Oboe,' Sir Malcolm demanded, 'did you hear me?'

Whittaker looked up, but still not quite at Sir Malcolm.

'What?' he asked of nobody in particular.

'Oboe,' Sir Malcolm tried again, 'did you hear me? You are flat.'

Whittaker looked down sharply at his instrument. 'Oboe,' he said, wagging his finger at the instrument, 'did you hear that, you beggar? You're flat.'

♪

Sir Malcolm Sargent was probably more conscious of his audience appeal than any other British conductor, and he took great pains to give
them what they wanted. From his starched collar
(which was stiff enough to support a broken
neck) to his white carnation, he looked the part.
Nothing was allowed to come between his care-
fully nurtured image and his admirers.

At a Promenade Concert in the Royal Albert
Hall during the early sixties, he finished a performance and left the stage to tremendous acclaim from his devoted Promenaders. With six
thousand people in the audience the evening was
hot and humid. Unfortunately, just as the conductor departed one of the backdesk violinists,
overcome by the heat, fell off his chair. As his
colleagues struggled, with instruments beneath
their arms and bows in their hands, to prop him
back onto his seat, Sir Malcolm turned to make
his way back to the rostrum to enjoy further
plaudits. From his place at the artists' entrance he
soon realised that some sort of disturbance was
taking place.

'What's going on?' he asked the BBC Symphony Orchestra's attendant. 'What's happening
over there?'

'I think someone's fainted, Sir Malcolm,' he
replied.

'What's he think he's doing?' the manicured

maestro demanded. 'He's simply going to ruin my second entrance.'

A LITTLE TROUBLE WITH THE LANGUAGE

The Russian conductor Serge Koussevitsky started out musical life as a virtuoso double-bass player, only taking up the baton for the first time in 1908 when he directed the London Symphony Orchestra. After the Revolution, when he managed to escape from the Soviet Union, he accepted an appointment with the Boston Symphony Orchestra. Uncommonly for a conductor, he retained a keen interest in new music even into old age (he died in 1951 at the age of seventy-seven), his most famous commission, in 1943, being Bartók's Concerto for Orchestra.

One of Koussevitsky's chief problems was his sketchy knowledge of the English (or American) language, and although his ignorance of its subtleties is understandable, the most famous story concerning this passionate man is still a little hard to swallow.

One day, in the course of a rehearsal, he had an argument with one of his players which degenerated into a row. He invited the offending musician to leave the platform. The player made his way angrily through the orchestra, watched the whole time by the irate conductor.

As he left the stage the player turned, looked the maestro firmly in the eye, and sneered out the current American word of abuse. 'Nuts.'

Koussevitsky straightened up, like a schoolmaster about to state the obvious. 'Already,' he began, 'it is too late to apologise.'

Probably the most enthusiastic conductor of contemporary music from the twenties to the fifties (when his enthusiasm for the *avant garde* seems to have deserted him) was the Swiss conductor Ernest Ansermet, a former professor of mathematics.

During his time with Diaghilev's Ballet Russe he conducted many notable performances of Stravinsky's great works. On one occasion in London his rehearsal of *Petroushka* was disturbed by a joke from one of the players in the orchestra.

Ansermet tried to get the rehearsal under way again, but there was still a certain amount of giggling going on, so he decided to stop it by using these classic words which were noted down on the spot by the orchestral pianist.

'Gentlemen!' he began. 'A joke then and now – yes! Very sometimes – but always – by God never!'

(This story, also concerning Ansermet, is sometimes told as having happened with the

BBC Symphony Orchestra in the 1950s, but I have chosen the earlier as being the more likely.)

♩

Paul Kletzki, the splendid Polish conductor, was sharing a tour with Sir John Barbirolli. Each had his own programmes to direct, with the exception of Elgar's Introduction and Allegro for Strings. As a result the orchestra was forced to learn two very different ways of playing the same work.

Kletzki approached the piece with no 'traditional' preconceptions. To him it was simply another work for string orchestra with no images of the Malvern Hills or Worcester to haunt him, no interpretative ideas received from previous generations.

Barbirolli, on the other hand, had been reared on performances of it since a boy and, although it would be foolish to suggest that his was a derivative interpretation, it cannot be denied that it rested on a solid bed of Englishness.

One evening Kletzki decided to go along to one of Barbirolli's concerts. He sat in the front row in full view of the orchestra. When Barbirolli began the Elgar, Kletzki's interest grew intense and, with the dramatic fugue in full flow, a frown appeared on his face.

Barbirolli treated the fugue with considerable

spaciousness, attending to each accent and giving each stress its full weight, while Kletzki was used to playing it with great fervour and snap. They were two very different realisations of the same score, but of similar quality.

When the concert ended, Kletzki went backstage to see Barbirolli. Poor Kletzki wanted to say how much he appreciated the bravery of someone prepared to hold such a dramatic work under such a disciplined rein and not lose control over it. But with his broken English, it came out all wrong.

'Sir John,' he began, his eyes blazing with an ambiguous intensity, 'how can you take the fugue so slow – I would not.'

Barbirolli, misreading the words for the intention, answered abruptly. 'Well, go home then.'

Many of the Philharmonia's players found Guido Cantelli's attitudes very childish – indeed, some of his behaviour was extraordinarily hard to swallow. His desire for tension was often carried to absurd lengths and he would fly off the handle at the least provocation.

On one occasion he called a halt in a rehearsal of a particular piece and the orchestra, with one exception, dutifully stopped playing. One player allowed the note he was playing to continue to fade away while the maestro was speaking.

'Oh, no,' Cantelli shouted in his most confused English, 'you have winded my prude.'

♪

The toweringly introspective German conductor Wilhelm Furtwängler was notorious for the vagueness of his beat. He found it particularly difficult actually to begin a work, especially one which held great mystical significance for him. A member of the London Philharmonic maintained that the real beat only began once Furtwängler had carried out a dozen or so introductory waggles of the baton.

Probably the best story of his method of rehearsing comes from the great cellist Gregor Piatigorsky, who watched him struggle to convey his wishes in language not unlike that heard a hundred times a day on radio phone-in programmes.

'Gentlemen, this phrase must be, must be . . . it must, it must . . . you know what I mean . . . please try it again . . . please.'

Afterwards he said to Piatigorsky, 'You see how important it is for a conductor to convey his wishes clearly?'

Despite all this, the relationship between conductor and orchestra is such that it can survive almost any barrier, even that of language. Interpreters often act as intermediaries and, in emergencies, there is always Italian, the international language of music, to save the day.

Sometimes, of course, relations can become overstrained, particularly if the conductor holds too high an opinion of his linguistic abilities. Over-confidence usually brings disaster.

The noted Italian conductor Fernando Previtali was in London to give a series of concerts with one of the major orchestras. The rehearsals began reasonably enough, but soon the players assumed one of their more boisterous moods.

As they challenged his authority, the maestro began to lose control. Inevitably his patience snapped, and the weakness of his command of the vernacular caused him to bring forth a jewel of misplaced confidence.

'You think I know damn nothing,' he screamed through the players' indifference, and then he straightened himself up with all the pride of the offended Latin. 'In fact – I know damn all.'

THE MAESTROS

Toscanini:
A Towering Inferno

Over the centuries most nationalities have been ascribed certain cliché characteristics which conductors often oblige their audiences by living up to. Even so, not all Germans are stolid and lacking in humour and not all Italians are emotional and operating on short fuses. Fortunately, though, enough of them fulfil our stock notions for us to hang on to our comforting preconceptions.

One conductor who was a curious amalgam of intellectual rigour and Italianate passion was Arturo Toscanini. His ruthless adherence to the letter of the score was legendary.

However, his single-minded devotion to the over-all master plan of the strictest German classical forms went hand in hand with outbursts of a total lack of emotional control.

One day he was rehearsing some singers and the soprano was giving him great trouble. No matter how hard he tried, he failed to get her to understand what he wanted. She seemed quite unable to interpret his instructions.

Apart from the quality of her voice, her only remarkable feature was the extreme ampleness of her bosom – what used to be known as a 'roll-top desk'.

Eventually Toscanini became so frustrated, so

bottled up with rage and fury at being denied the release which only artistic perfection can bring, that he dashed onto the stage and seized her by her largest assets, yelling, 'If only these were brains.'

♩

On another notable occasion he was struggling with an American soprano whose voice was considerably more magnificent than her intellect. The great maestro spent hours trying to get her to perform in the way he wanted but, alas, to no avail. In the end he simply gave up and lost his temper, treating her to his most abusive Italian insults and ranting and raving at her, while she simply stood and stared at him, uncomprehending.

When he had finished, she turned to her immediate colleague to ask what he had been shouting about. She had failed to make any connection between her own singing and his raging. Toscanini stomped off, still furious.

'The voice is so 'igh,' he muttered, 'there is no room for the brain in the 'ead.'

♩

During the 1930s Toscanini visited London on a couple of occasions to conduct the superb new BBC Symphony Orchestra. He was widely regarded as being 'the best conductor in the world' – the sort of naïve judgement which has, thankfully, now gone out of fashion.

All sorts of people hung about the great man during rehearsals and concerts. Sir John Barbirolli, whose own conducting ideals seemed so different from the maestro's, was one young aspirant who waited on him during these visits.

One day, in the green room, Barbirolli watched Toscanini work himself into a towering rage. He stormed round the room, shouting and banging furniture in a genuine passion. Barbirolli wondered why he was so out of control.

At last the reason became clear. One of General Franco's Fascist generals had been killed that morning in a plane crash.

'But Mussolini,' screamed the disappointed Toscanini, 'he keeps on flying. Nothing kills 'im.'

♩

William Primrose was the foremost viola player of his day and for some time was principal in Toscanini's orchestra, the New York Philharmonic.

In common with so many of Toscanini's players, he had a mixture of fear and affection for the fiery and demanding maestro. Toscanini seemed rarely to indulge in small talk or to make conversation for its own sake.

Consequently one can imagine Primrose's surprise and delight when Toscanini called out to him one day, 'Primrose, my wife, she is away. You come and 'ave dinner with me at 'ome tonight.'

What an honour, thought Primrose, what a chance to talk to the greatest conductor in the world in peace and quiet. He would be able to talk to him about Verdi, to ask him about the first night of *Otello*, to discuss his early days as a cellist, hear how he was snatched from the pit totake up the stick without notice and save the production.

When Primrose reached Toscanini's house the butler let him in. Dinner was served and Toscanini tore his way through a platter of spaghetti and drained his glass with a minimum of fuss. There was still no talk. Perhaps, thought Primrose, they would get down to the discussion once the food had been cleared away.

But no. As soon as the meal was finished, the greatest conductor in the world rushed into an adjoining room and switched on the television. Was it to be a TV broadcast of some mighty opera? Or a programme of Mozart string quintets? No, it was wrestling. There he sat, in front of the TV set, shouting his head off with delighted partisan advice.

'Hit 'im in de stommak. Twist off 'is leg. Breaka 'is arm. Stampa on 'im.'

It wasn't quite what Primrose had expected.

♩

When a memorial service was held for Toscanini shortly after his death, a little violinist who had been a long-suffering member of the maestro's NBC Symphony Orchestra went to the orchestra's office for a ticket. He was told that all the tickets had gone. He looked disappointed, even dejected.

'I'm really so sorry,' the woman in the office said to him, 'you used to play for the maestro, didn't you?'

'Yes,' he replied sadly. Then he brightened. 'Still,' he continued, 'if I can't have one for Toscanini's memorial service can you save me one for Szell's?'

Klemperer:
The Indomitable

One of the problems facing any younger generation is the difficulty of envisaging what an older person was like in earlier times. During our formative years we are prone to believe that people were always the way they now seem to be.

How hard it is for us who remember him only from his last years to imagine Otto Klemperer ever being young! He seemed to have been around for ever. His interpretations gave the impression of having been handed down on tablets from on high, as though conceived within the timeless limitations of eternity.

Yet, like everyone else, he must have been young at some time, and there are photographs of him from before the last war which show him as a fine, virile and dominating personality.

Many years ago Klemperer made his way briskly to the centre of the concert platform. No sooner had he arrived at the rostrum than a man from the audience approached him as he was bowing to the initial applause and struck him a savage blow to the face.

Unabashed, Klemperer rose to his full height of well over six feet and, overcoming the buzz of excitement from the shocked audience, announced in a confident voice, 'Ladies and gentlemen! The wife of the gentleman who has just struck me has today consented to become my mistress!'

The music publishers Schott and Co. have an office over their ground-floor shop. One morning, many years ago, the manager of the shop, looking rather harassed, went up to the office.

'There's a man downstairs who wants to know why we haven't got his music in stock. He says we publish it.'

At that point a giant figure blocked out the light in the doorway.

'Why haven't you my music?' the figure demanded.

'I'm sorry, sir. What's your name?'

'Klemperer,' came the reply.

Schott's office staff had no idea that Klemperer was a composer or that they were supposed to be his publisher. They backed off with many apologies. One of them went in search of the managing director. Perhaps he would know about it.

Unfortunately the managing director was unsure which of the many conductors whose names began with K he had in the outer office. It might have been Kleiber, Knappertsbusch, Keilberth or Krips, for all he cared. He rummaged through some old papers, scratching his head.

'Do you know, I think we sent it all up to his wife, during the war,' he suggested to his assistant, 'she was in Lancashire – I think.'

The assistant, clutching at this unlikely theory, returned to the intimidating presence of the giant composer/conductor and decided to smooth the way by explaining it in German.

Unfortunately, when he got to the bit about his music having been sent to his wife somewhere in darkest Lancashire, he used the word *'Weib'*, instead of a more correct German word for wife, *'Frau'*.

With a great bellow of laughter the massive figure rocked on its feet at the joke. 'I've had women all over the world. Lots of 'em,' he roared, 'but never, never in Lancashire.'

♩

After some years, the leader of the Philharmonia Orchestra resigned. He had decided that a solo career away from orchestras would be best for his future development. He had played for all the great conductors from Furtwängler to Von Karajan, and he felt himself in increasing danger of merely repeating himself.

The battered yet heroic Otto Klemperer was one conductor with whom he felt he had developed a particular rapport. Under his rock-like direction the Philharmonia had given concerts which set new standards of interpretation.

The rehearsals for the leader's final concert came and went. All that remained was the concert itself. As he drove through the darkened London streets, he thought how sad it was to be leaving such close colleagues and, especially, to be near the end of his ripe relationship with Klemperer. He felt compelled to go to the maestro before the concert, and to express these feelings. He would then feel that he had dotted the i's and crossed the t's of an association which meant so much to him and, he hoped, to Klemperer too.

He entered the Royal Festival Hall and took the artists' lift backstage. He sought out the conductor's room and knocked. He entered. There was the great man, in his stiff white shirt, awaiting his call.

'Maestro,' the leader began, 'I thought I ought to come and see you before the concert tonight. Do you know how many years it's been since we started working together? It's been a long time – a wonderful time. It's been marvellous working with you. A privilege. And now it's our last concert together. I just felt I must tell you how much it's meant to me.'

The venerable conductor cocked his head to one side, eyeing the man before him as though he were an old bird of prey examining his next meal.

'What do you want me to do?' he demanded. 'Weep?'

♪

In 1959, when old and tired, Klemperer set fire to himself while smoking in bed. He looked round for some water to throw on the flames and saw a flask by his side. He emptied its contents onto the burning bedding and over himself.

Disastrously, the flask contained not water but spirit of camphor. He was badly burned and had to spend many weeks convalescing. However, his own spirit was genuinely indomitable and he returned to conducting – although, rather foolishly, he did so before the wounds had had a chance to heal properly.

His reappearance was greeted by the orchestra with respect, and even affection. Everyone was impressed by his courage and dignity in coping with such a dreadful accident at his age.

'How are you, maestro?' the leader inquired as the old man clambered onto the platform for his first rehearsal. 'We all hope you will soon be fully recovered.'

Klemperer hesitated for a moment before fixing his eyes on the leader's face.

'They don't seem to understand,' he grumbled in disbelief at his doctor's lack of comprehension, 'that I won't really heal properly until I start making music.'

♪

A severely Teutonic conductor, Klemperer was

once directing a recording of Bach's mighty *St Matthew Passion*. By the time of the recording, the early 1960s, he was already an old man and had little experience of the increasingly fashionable use of harpsichords in performing the continuo (a bass line, left by baroque composers, for the performers to elaborate). In any case he could see no reason why he should deviate from Bach's bald text.

George Malcolm, who had been engaged for the recording, was Britain's foremost harpsichordist and accustomed to playing extempore on an instrument whose many changes of registration allowed him to conjure a multiplicity of tone colours from it with ease.

No sooner had he begun to add his characteristically florid embellishments to Bach's simple original than Klemperer turned on him.

'Do not joke with Bach,' he commanded.

♩

However, although Klemperer was renowned for his adherence to the letter of the text in Bach and Beethoven, for example, his standards, in common with those of many other interpreters, became far more flexible with Handel. As a result he made numerous cuts and even left out entire items.

At a concert performance of Handel's *Messiah*

in the Royal Festival Hall, George Malcolm was seated at his harpsichord in the centre of the stage, directly in front of the conductor's rostrum. The first few items went well, and the team of world-class soloists, Philharmonia Orchestra and Chorus performed impeccably, until they reached a point where Klemperer forgot to observe one of his own cuts.

He waved an arm at George Malcolm, thinking that the harpsichord should be playing the opening chords of a recitative. Nothing happened. Malcolm looked at his music and kept his eyes averted. Again the venerable figure swung a gnarled hand at the apparently indifferent harpsichordist. Again his gesture was ignored.

The concert was being broadcast. Many seconds had passed since the end of the previous item. The players in the orchestra knew that Klemperer had made a mistake, but what could they do? They could scarcely speak and have their voices picked up by the radio. Microphones were everywhere. The BBC engineers began to move restlessly in their glass-bound box. The continuity announcer could be seen rustling his papers. The audience began to sense things were not right.

After two or three minutes of complete inactivity, Dr Klemperer leaned forward.

'Mr Malcolm, you must play,' he growled.

Malcolm shrugged his shoulders. He might have been waiting for a bus. The orchestra sat

fascinated by this duel, intrigued to see its out-
come. However, the leader, taking a broader
view, decided enough was enough and rose from
his seat to whisper the number of the next item in
the stiff-faced conductor's ear.

Sadly, Klemperer was deaf in his left ear and
failed to hear the leader's words. Everyone else
sat still and did nothing to help. Finally the leader
moved to the front of the rostrum, into Klemperer's line of vision, and as the concert continued he
was looking at his harpsichordist with new eyes.

♪

Klemperer enjoyed an astonishing Indian
summer as a conductor. Year after year every
London season seemed to have a cycle of Beethoven's symphonies under his direction. He
became an institution, apparently possessed of
superhuman power.

He alone seemed to hold the thread of communication between Beethoven's intentions and
the audience. Nothing was allowed to come between his insights and his execution.

On one particular occasion when he came out
onto the podium at the start of a concert in the
Royal Festival Hall the violinists on the front
desk noticed with a mixture of surprise and
horror that Dr Klemperer's flies were undone.

With much expressive rolling of his eyes, the

leader attempted to indicate the nature of the potential embarrassment to his conductor, who by that time had taken his place on his seat. But to no avail. Klemperer remained uncomprehending.

Until, at last, unable to ignore the winking and gesticulating of a normally sensible man, he leaned down to ask what he was up to.

'Your flies are undone,' the leader whispered.

Klemperer looked nonplussed.

'What's that got to do with Beethoven?' he growled dismissively.

In the sixties Klemperer's records of Beethoven enjoyed a rare unanimity of critical acclaim throughout the world. Most of his concerts were given in London. There must have been thou-

sands of music lovers at that time who would have given anything to have heard just one concert under the master's authoritative guidance.

Such a man lived in South Africa. He had bought all Klemperer's records and had listened to them so often that eventually he decided he must go to London to hear Beethoven's music come to life under his hero's hands. Unfortunately he was far from rich. He scrimped and saved to pay for his flight and scanned the London concert lists to choose the best programme.

Then, he did a remarkable thing, for such a mild person. He wrote to Klemperer to ask if he might visit him backstage after the concert. Klemperer's secretary replied that it would be perfectly all right.

On the evening of the concert, she told the great conductor of the little man from South Africa, and of how he had struggled to make such a long and expensive journey to hear Klemperer's Beethoven in the Royal Festival Hall.

'Just think,' she said, 'what it must mean to him. He's come all that way and saved so hard. Please be kind to him when he turns up. Say something to him, won't you?'

The old man looked at her, but said nothing.

By the time the concert had finished, the South African was completely overwhelmed by the nobility of the experience. It was far better than any recording. He was uplifted and elated by the heady atmosphere. He went backstage and found the door with Klemperer's name on it. He knocked. The door opened. There stood Klemperer's secretary.

'Mr Van Der Weele?' she asked.

The man nodded, unable to speak, for sitting at the back of the room was Dr Otto Klemperer, the great conductor. The interpreter of Beethoven for an entire generation. A man he had never dared hope to meet.

The secretary motioned him to enter.

'Here's the gentleman I was telling you about – from South Africa. Please say something to him. He's come such a long way to meet you.'

Dr Klemperer thrust out a horny hand, his old eyes glistening, and took Mr Van Der Weele's hand in his.

'Goodbye,' he said.

♩

At a concert in the Royal Festival Hall Klemperer, by then well into his eighties, struggled painfully onto the rostrum and took his place on a high stool in front of the orchestra.

He had endured several strokes and his legs were wretchedly weak. His mouth pulled hard to one side, especially when he spoke. His eyes ran with dampness down each side of an aquiline nose.

Dr Klemperer's progress to the podium had

been engulfed in that especially rapturous applause which the English reserve for the exceptionally old and highly revered. The orchestra, too, joined in the celebration of his arrival at the centre of the stage. Only he, the object of all this adulation, appeared less than delighted.

The audience were stilled, waiting for the mysteries of the great German classics to be laid open to them by the needle-sharp intellect of the grand old man.

He sat motionless for a few moments. Then he began to bend gently downwards in the direction of the leader, who watched as the twisted form of the venerable conductor inclined in his direction.

Klemperer's mouth began to move, as though he were struggling to summon sufficient momentum in his jaw to speak. But what was he about to say? What important message was he about to impart? And at such a point in a concert.

The leader half rose from his chair, his violin held gently beneath his arm. Klemperer continued to lean down still further until his mouth was close to the leader's blushing ear. His mouth opened, he took a breath.

'What a life,' he muttered.

Eccentrics and Geniuses

At the turn of the century the young Clemens Kraus was invited to conduct the mighty Vienna Philharmonic Orchestra. He was overawed at the prospect of first rehearsal.

When he came to stand on the box, facing nearly a hundred men who had played for all the great maestros of the previous forty years or so, he was terribly nervous. He looked at the score. It was a Brahms symphony. He raised his arms and the orchestra raised their instruments. With a conscious effort he brought his arms down on the first beat and they were off, in strong pursuit of the music's content.

He struggled to find something to say, something which would make a real contribution to the performance of this great work. But his head swam with the majesty of the sound produced by an orchestra already steeped in Brahms' unique sonorities.

The first movement passed, and Kraus had found nothing he dared mention. The second and third movements followed equally smoothly, although the stick was becoming loose in his sweaty grip.

The last movement was reached, but still no word had passed his lips.

'I've got to say something,' he said to himself,

'but what? It all seems so good – and I mustn't make a fool of myself!'

Suddenly, he had an idea. Why not ask the first horn to stress the top note of the phrase which had just passed? He stopped the orchestra and, blushing and stammering, gave his instructions. The horn player altered his part with a pencil.

Soon the rehearsal was at an end. The young conductor retreated to his room and lay on his bed with weak knees. At least he had managed to get through the ordeal. He had made a genuine contribution to the rehearsal – and no one had laughed at him.

There came a tap at the door.

The head which came round the door belonged to the grey-haired horn player.

'Maestro,' he said quietly, 'you know that place you asked me to accent?'

'Yes,' said Kraus, proud of his insight in having drawn attention to it, 'what about it?'

'Well, when we used to do it for Dr Brahms he always made a point of telling us to play that bit as smoothly as possible. That's all. Of course, if you really want me to . . .'

♩

Albert Coates was of Anglo-Russian parentage. By the time of the 1917 revolution he was thirty-five and had already made a name for himself in several German opera houses directing Mozart, Wagner and Strauss. He had also conducted the London Symphony Orchestra and achieved considerable success in his native St Petersburg. He had been educated in England, so he found coping with a totalitarian regime something of a trial.

Before managing to escape from the Soviet Union in 1919, Coates directed several concerts for the leaders of the new order. At the end of one performance he was taken to task by Stalin for his choice of music.

'It is not politically strong,' Stalin declared.

'Why do you say that to me?' Coates demanded. 'I wouldn't accuse you of having unmusical politics.'

♩

Rudolf Schwarz came to England after the Second World War, having suffered terribly in Hitler's Germany. His youth had been spent in a Vienna which still echoed to the sounds of imperial Austria.

Schwarz's brother was working in Norwich, and had seen an advertisement by the Bournemouth Corporation for a conductor. He sent it to Schwarz, who was in Sweden at the time recuperating from his wartime ordeals.

Musical opinion in England has always tended

to be impressed by sheer quantity. Whereas conductors in Europe were expected to give some fifty concerts a year, in Britain they had to cope with four times that number. Musical life in old Vienna must have possessed a good deal more casual charm even than old Bournemouth.

When Schwarz was shown the list of two hundred concerts to be given in the first year by the reconstructed Bournemouth Orchestra, he wanted to know who the other conductors would be.

'You,' the manager told him, 'you are the other conductors.'

'But what if I get ill?' Schwarz wanted to know.

'You will not get ill,' the manager ordered. 'Bournemouth is a very healthy place.'

♩

In the 1950s conductors still felt able to misbehave without much fear of being disciplined. One such was the gifted, but hugely temperamental, Guido Cantelli, the most talented pupil of Toscanini.

Cantelli's very first rehearsal with the Philharmonia got off to a bad start. They were rehearsing Strauss's tone poem *Tod und Verklärung*, and immediately the flautist, Gareth Morris, fell foul of the maestro. Just as he was bringing the instrument to his lips for his first entry, Cantelli snapped, 'It must be *piano* – *pianissimo.*'

'How can it be any quieter?' Morris asked. 'I haven't even begun to play a note.'

Cantelli's response was to leave the rostrum and not to return.

♩

Some twenty years later a highly regarded oboe player, then in the twilight of his playing career, walked into a recording studio in west London. Sitting in a corner, minding his own business, was a colleague from their days in the Philharmonia, days when the orchestra was directed by the very best in the world, including the errant Cantelli.

'Do you remember,' the oboist began, 'when we did that *Daphnis and Chloë* with Cantelli?'

'Yes,' replied the trumpet player, 'I remember.'

'Do you remember how he nearly ripped the control room door off its hinges, because he got so angry with us? Said we were the worst orchestra he'd ever had to conduct.'

'Yes,' agreed the trumpeter.

'I'll never forget how he came out from a playback and said the second fiddles should all be taken out and shot.'

'Didn't he lie on the floor and beat a tattoo with his heels, screaming his head off?' asked the trumpeter, entering into the spirit. 'And didn't he rip his music to pieces because he said he'd never settle for anything less than absolute perfection?'

The oboe player smiled broadly.

'That's the chap.'

'Why?' asked the trumpeter. 'What about it?'

'Oh, I just saw a copy in the Portobello Road for 45 pence.'

♩

Leopold Stokowski was born in St John's Wood and, before finding fame and fortune in the United States, was organist of St James's Church, Piccadilly. He was away from England for many years and, during his absence in North America, picked up a curious sort of central European accent. He also, apparently, forgot a surprising amount of information concerning substantial items of national heritage.

While on his way from the Royal Festival Hall with the chairman and manager of the London Symphony Orchestra, he peered out of the limousine's window and looked up at Big Ben's imposing clock tower as they crossed Westminster Bridge.

'Big clock,' he exclaimed, in his central European newspeak, 'what is called?'

♩

Franz Reizenstein was engaged to play Beethoven's 'Emperor' Concerto with an orchestra

under the direction of Josef Krips. Although normally a fine pianist, throughout the rehearsal he played a fistful of wrong notes.

The players looked at each other in trepidation. Krips either buried his head in the score or stared into the middle distance.

When the performance itself arrived, Reizenstein managed to strike more than his fair share of wrong notes, until at the end the orchestra shuffled off the platform wondering how any audience could have found so much to applaud.

Krips mopped his normally pink Viennese face, now a deep shade of red, with a large handkerchief. Up bounced the beaming soloist.

'What do you think of me now, Josef?' he asked proudly.

Members of the orchestra leaned forward, eager to hear what gem of diplomacy would fall from the maestro's lips.

'The trouble is this, dear friend,' he said, 'there are always witnesses to a musical murder.'

♩

Karl Böhm was a great friend of Richard Strauss. Indeed, the great arch-romantic had dedicated several works to his staunch admirer. They had a lot in common. John Culshaw, the splendid record producer, told me of an occasion when the Decca office was visited by Erich Kleiber, who saw his photograph hanging between those of Clemens Kraus and Karl Böhm.

'You're not going to have my picture hanging between those two old Nazis!' he declared and had their positions changed.

On another occasion, when the London Symphony Orchestra wished to have Böhm appointed principal conductor in place of André Previn, they had his photograph specially framed and mounted with the signatures of 99 per cent of the players surrounding it.

The orchestra's managing director had the task of making the presentation to the old man during a visit to Salzburg, and of sounding him out with regard to his taking up the appointment.

'What's the frame like?' the managing director asked the concerts manager when she arrived with the frame in Salzburg.

'It's very nice,' she said, 'it's made of stainless steel.'

'Good!' he replied. 'It'll match his teeth!'

The young Riccardo Muti was rehearsing the London Symphony Orchestra in a work close to any Italian's heart – Verdi's *Requiem*. The intensity with which he went about his business in strange surroundings, so different from those of his native Italy, was much admired by the players – although, it has to be admitted, orchestral players are not necessarily at their most sensitive when rehearsing.

The end of the rehearsals approached and Muti, feeling that he should bare his innermost thoughts, tried to explain the profound nature of his sentiments.

'This work,' he began, haltingly, 'means so much to me. I played it for my . . .' and here he paused. 'For my mother-in-law.'

At this the orchestra collapsed in uncontrolled laughter. Soon afterwards, Mr Muti began working with the Philharmonia Orchestra where, perhaps, music hall jokes concerning mothers-in-law were less well known.

♪

As principal conductor of the Philharmonia Orchestra Muti soon developed a rapport with his new audience – an absolute essential for conducting success.

A conductor needs to have complete confidence in his players. Once, when conducting a Schubert Symphony, he reached the minuet which, in typically Schubertian fashion, had a contrasting trio section in its middle. The trouble was that the trio comes round several times, and people have been known to get lost and to forget exactly how many times they have played it.

In this instance the maestro did miscount and, when he thought he had finished with the trio, he raised his arms and beat savagely in the air as though about to introduce the louder music of the minuet. Sadly, he was all alone, for the orchestra paid not a jot of attention to him but continued with the gentle trio until they arrived at the minuet proper.

Next day Muti stood in front of the orchestra. 'You followed me so well,' he declared and, wishing not to be left out of any credit for the Philharmonia's avoidance of disaster, 'because, because I trained you so well.'

♪

Lorin Maazel, whose prodigious memory is

widely discussed, was in London's Royal Albert Hall rehearsing the Philharmonia Orchestra in Mahler's mighty Second Symphony.

It is composed on a vast scale, lasting some eighty minutes, and requires a huge orchestra, female soloists and as big a choir as can be assembled. The number of notes in the score is almost incalculable. The sheer, physical effort in actually writing them all down would rival the work-rate of a Dickens.

At one point, in the midst of this titanic work, the contra-bassoonist, Norman Reader, looked over his music-stand at the conductor who, as is his custom, was rehearsing without music.

'Should this be a B natural or a B flat?' he asked.

Maazel closed his eyes, while the orchestra waited and watched, marvelling at such a sight. He stood, thinking hard as the pages of the score passed in sequence before the searchlight of his inner self, until, with a look of recognition, he exclaimed, 'B flat.'

♩

Yehudi Menuhin, one of this century's finest and most natural talents, first came to England to record Elgar's violin concerto under the composer's own direction. The young Menuhin had the sort of natural genius which comes but rarely and, in pursuit of his own fulfilment, he had given up most of his young life to practising the violin.

The teenager was taken to play for the old composer, who was now in his eighties. No sooner had he played a few bars than Elgar stood up and announced that he was off to the races. Such apparent indifference to his craft amazed the violinist.

In recent years Menuhin has increasingly taken to conducting, and he now appears with orchestras across the world. Despite the many opportunities for broadening his awareness of the full extent of human nature, which come the way of anyone mixing with orchestral players, it has to be admitted that Sir Yehudi has contrived to retain the innocence of his youth.

Once, when conducting the Royal Philharmonic Orchestra, he wanted a sudden quietness at a specific place in the music. 'Can we all go down at 69?' he asked.

♩

During the early 1990s the Philharmonia Orchestra was being conducted, in the Royal Festival Hall, by the noted Russian conductor, Evgeni Svetlanov. The concert ended with one of his favourite works, Rachmaninoff's Second Symphony. This lengthy work is filled to overflowing with the introspective musings of the committed romantic and Svetlanov rose to the challenge superbly.

The players, drained by their efforts, watched the audience rise in spontaneous acclaim of a performance rarely equalled in living memory. However, the conductor left the podium at some speed and returned only a split second later for the first of many anticipated curtain calls. The audience applauded in their delirium at having identified a great performance and were keen to display their enthusiasm. The Philharmonia remained seated, clapping the conductor, with equal gratitude.

But, what was this? The conductor was taking the orchestra's leader by the arm and had begun propelling him from the stage, followed, as is the inevitable custom, by the rest of the orchestra. The audience looked askance as they watched their heroes deserting them.

As they left the stage, Svetlanov whispered to the leader a message of deep significance. What could explain his dash from the stage, at the point in a concert often most enjoyed by performers?

'I'm not going to miss the snooker final,' he said, 'it's on television. There's no time to waste.'

SHOW-BIZ AND OPERA HOUSES

Most orchestras have their resident complainers, people who can be relied on to bitch about a catalogue of standard orchestral grievances. For instance, unless the music is brand new, someone is almost certain to protest about the impossibility of reading it.

When they do eventually stop carping about the music, they turn their attention to the unsuitability of the temperature, or the fact that the lights are too bright or too dim, or, most fashionably, that they hum.

The reason for such tetchiness is seldom obvious. It may stem from problems at home, or the player may be going through a rough patch with his playing and feel the need to put the boot in before someone gets at him. The conductor must keep an eye open for such signs of unrest if he is to maintain control of his players and produce music of the required standard.

Bernard Hermann, the American film music composer, had seen a good deal of the hard face of orchestral life during his years in the tough world of Hollywood. He had a Bronx accent and a voice like barbed wire. He was once rehearsing the

LSO in a recording. Soon after they began, he stopped the orchestra when it was in full spate.

'Why didn't you play?' he demanded of the flutes and oboes. 'Don't you wanna play wid us? Ain't we good enough for you?'

Quick as a flash they came back at him, confident that the composer had misread his own score. 'There's nothing here for us to play,' they exclaimed, pointing at the music.

'You're kidding,' Hermann replied. 'Have another look.'

The four players leaned forward and scrutinised the manuscript with increased intensity.

'Yes,' muttered one of the squinting oboists grudgingly, 'there is something here.'

'So there is,' agreed the other, adding with scorn as though all the rules of civilised behaviour were being ignored, 'but it's written in pencil.'

Hermann sat relaxed on his high conductor's stool and raised his arms in a gesture of supplication.

'These guys. What do they expect?' he wondered out loud. 'Neon lights?'

♪

In the late 1950s Leonard Bernstein's most notable work, *West Side Story*, was due to open

for the first time in the West End. The promoters, naturally enough, wanted the best possible orchestra in the pit.

One of the most accomplished jazz drummers
in London was Phil Seaman. He was asked to
play for the opening few weeks of the production
and he agreed, but on one condition – that he
could have his dog with him.

The management argued with him, pointing
out the requirements of the byelaws, but he continued to insist on being accompanied by his dog.
Eventually they capitulated and swore the rest of
the players to secrecy.

An American conductor had been engaged to
direct this star-studded orchestra. When the rehearsals began Seaman was sitting at one end of
the pit, surrounded by a comprehensive drum
kit, the dog's lead trapped beneath a chairleg.
Soon after the beginning of the first rehearsal, the
dog yelped. The conductor looked up.

'A dog,' he exclaimed, 'I heard a dog.'

The players looked at each other.

'You did hear a dog, didn't you?' he inquired, a
little anxiously.

'A dog?' queried a saxophone player, 'what
dog?'

'I didn't hear a thing,' confirmed a trumpeter.

The conductor looked bemused. Slowly he
took up his baton and began uncertainly to rehearse again.

The next day the dog barked again. But the
players continued to deny any knowledge of its

100

existence. Only the conductor seemed able to hear the phantom canine. Some days and several barks later, the conductor felt so uneasy about his mental state that he began visiting a psychiatrist to discuss this worrying new problem. The wretched man spent hours delving into the half-remembered days of his childhood.

However, soon after *West Side Story* opened, in the middle of a public performance the dog decided to free himself from his drumming owner and to speed the length of the pit in pursuit of an innocent trombonist's leg. As he ran between the musicians' chairs he gave little yelps of delight. The conductor looked down, fearing for his sanity. But when he saw a real dog and heard the sharp cry of pain from the lips of the assaulted trombonist, he tossed his baton high in the air and threw up his arms in gratitude.

'A dog,' he yelled with relief, 'there is a dog. I knew there was a dog.'

♩

Not all conductors are classical authorities and not all classical musicians play only classical music. Indeed, there is and probably always will be a middle ground between the extremes of jazz and the classics which offers many musicians rich pickings.

There used to be an extremely popular BBC

radio series which ran for many years, called 'Old Time Dancing'. These shows were directed by a splendid character, Harry Davidson, whose knowledge of more formal music was neither broad nor deep, but who nevertheless had a very clear understanding of what would prove marketable.

His orchestra consisted largely of first-class freelance players. Some, notably the wind, came from a nucleus of symphonic musicians capable of sustaining popular tunes with a consummate sense of line.

A particular early evening broadcast had attracted a cellist from one of the main London orchestras. Because he had to be at the Royal Festival Hall for that evening's concert, he had gone to the studio in his tail coat and was sitting incongruously among the other musicians dressed in ordinary suits.

When Davidson arrived, baton in hand, he did not fail to notice the elegance of the cellist's white tie and tails.

'We are honoured tonight,' he said with sarcastic humility. 'Where are we orf to when we've done our bit of slumming here? A spot of waiting at the Savoy, perhaps?'

'No,' the cellist replied stiffly, 'I'm on with the LSO at the Festival Hall!'

'Oh, really?' wondered Harry, 'wotcha doing? The Erocica?'[sic]

♪

One of the greatest conductors of Wagner was

Hans Knappertsbusch. He was notorious for the strict economy of his conducting style. He said little in rehearsal and barely moved his stick in performance, and it was said that he only needed to flick his cufflinks at the orchestra for the heavens to open.

Knappertsbusch had so much faith in himself and in his players that, when directing the season at Bayreuth, he only bothered to rehearse tempo changes and left the performance to gather its own momentum on the night.

In 1955 he directed the first three performances of *Der Fliegende Holländer*, while Josef Keilberth took the rest. The title role in most of the performances was sung by Hermann Uhde.

Uhde found one passage in Act II rather tricky so, during Keilberth's first full rehearsal, he took special care to see that he sang it correctly. But he was surprised and annoyed when he reached it to hear Keilberth begin to howl with laughter.

The rehearsal stopped and Uhde dashed to the front of the stage to find out what was going on. Keilberth apologised profusely. Then he pointed to what Knappertsbusch had written in the score:

'At this point the stupid twit cocks it up.'

André Previn has a wonderful way with words. He is never short of the apt phrase, the cutting edge, which survival in Hollywood demands.

Once in Hollywood, when he was directing a recording of Prokofiev's ballet *Cinderella* with his favourite orchestra, the LSO, the cello section was called upon to sing a particularly glorious melody. However, the maestro thought their corporate tone and phrasing were simply too rich in the context of the work and, understanding the rigours and demands of life in an orchestra, he turned to them with this insight into Cinderella's lifestyle.

'Not so sexy, you guys. This chick's never been on tour.'

Switzerland has produced a number of fine conductors but none more talented than Peter Maag.
He has worked a great deal in Italy and has been
chief conductor of the opera in Turin. Italian
orchestras are not the most open to discipline;
indeed, at the approach of a difficult solo in the
middle of a recording session they think nothing
of trying to renegotiate their fees.

One evening the Turin Opera Orchestra
decided to hold everybody to ransom. Argu-
ments between players and management over
fees had been going on for some time. Now, with
the audience already in their seats and waiting for
the curtain to rise, the orchestra refused to play
unless their demands were met.

'Fine,' declared Maag, determined not to bar-
ter under such pressure, 'do as you please.'

He then marched onto the stage and told the
audience what had been going on. He was treated
to an angry reception until he managed to add
that the performance would continue – for he and
a repetiteur would play the entire orchestral accompaniment on two pianos. Cries of support
filled the auditorium. The players' bluff had been
called.

The orchestra, having been made to look
pretty ungracious, asked to be allowed to play,
but Maag would have none of it. The performance was acclaimed as a great coup for sanity.
(The orchestra had gone home, so they didn't clap.)

The first night of the 1981 revival of Verdi's *Un Ballo in Maschera* at the Royal Opera House, Covent Garden, was somewhat troubled. The original tenor and baritone had failed to turn up.

At the end of the Act II trio, the Amelia, Montserrat Caballé, left the stage instead of remaining for her scene with Renato. The curtain descended.

The conductor, Bernard Haitink, picked up the phone in the pit to find out what was happening. The switchboard answered.

'Haitink here. Give me the stage manager.'

The switchboard replied, 'I'm sorry; I can't do that – there's a performance going on.'

Haitink looked up at the deep red and brilliant gold of the curtains. 'That's what you think,' he said, putting down the phone.

THE TRIALS OF COMPOSERS

The problem of introducing new music to audiences has become steadily worse for many years and, indeed, now seems insoluble as composers strive for originality at the expense of communication. The irony is that the greater the means of expression available in the concert hall, the less appears to be communicated.

In common with politicians, lawyers and doctors, composers generally support each other when under attack from outsiders, although, as with the other professions, they have been known to set about each other.

At the turn of the century Schoenberg was beginning to become well known and had written his String Quartet No. 1 in D minor. Fortunately for him, it was taken up by the famous Rose Quartet, although it received a hostile reception at its first performance.

Sitting in the audience was Gustav Mahler (at that time best known as a conductor), who had himself suffered a good deal at the hands of the conservative Viennese. He turned to one of the people hissing the loudest and told him to stop.

'There's no need to get excited,' the man replied. 'I hiss Mahler too.'

♪

Composers are seldom good interpreters of their own works. They seem to lack the quality of salesmanship so essential to the conductor's armoury. Vaughan Williams avoided most pitfalls by instructing orchestras under his direction, 'You start and I'll follow.'

Sir William Walton had a similar problem, but not such a straightforward solution. He was a kindly man who composed passionate and sometimes surprisingly ferocious music. One of the movements of his First Symphony is marked *con malizia*, an attitude of mind difficult to associate with his own gentle demeanour (especially when he apparently maintained after every performance of his own works that it was the best he had ever heard).

In the late 1950s Walton was conducting a recording of his highly charged oratorio *Belshazzar's Feast*. At one point he was absent from the rostrum listening to a playback of the sections already recorded.

The chorus master was the extraordinarily gifted Wilhelm Pitz. He had raised the Philharmonia Choir to unknown heights of corporate virtuosity and tone, and was quite incapable of sitting idly by and wasting valuable time during the conductor's absence. If time was available to move still nearer to perfection, he would use it.

As a result the choir were hard at it when Walton returned. He stood listening intently as he heard his own creation of thirty years before being newly forged under the impact of Pitz's amazing understanding. It was thrilling and brilliant.

As soon as Pitz noticed that the composer had returned, he vacated the podium. Sir William reluctantly took his place and stood, a rather small figure, in front of the massed orchestra, off-stage bands and choir, his pallid face now more saddened.

'Why can't you do it like that for me?' he asked.

The composer Zoltan Kodaly had to use an interpreter to convey his wishes to the orchestras he rehearsed in foreign countries. In common with most educated Hungarians he was fluent in German, so it was in that language that he conducted rehearsals during a trip to the United States.

On one occasion, at a point of intense frustration, Kodaly screamed, *'Schweinhunden! Sie spielen wie Schweinhunden!'*

The interpreter pondered for a moment, considering the many alternatives open to him, and then announced: 'Gentlemen, the maestro admires your playing very much indeed. But he'd like it better still if you would only give him a bit more expression at letter G!'

Sir Arthur Bliss was not the sort of man to suffer fools gladly. He had been a Guards officer in the First World War and, in common with many of his contemporaries, maintained a brisk no-nonsense surface somewhat at odds with an inner sensitivity. He was never likely to wear his heart on his sleeve.

Walter Legge was a recording manager with EMI. He had formed the Philharmonia Orchestra at the end of the Second War and had made it arguably the finest orchestra this country has ever produced.

He was a martinet in the studio, holding supreme power at a time before classical records could rely on the profits from pop records to subsidise them. As a result, he tended to adopt a dictatorial approach, whereas perhaps these days he might have been forced to employ stealthier methods to gain his ends.

He assumed an air of particular importance when recording with his orchestra, which they, being in his pay, were perfectly ready to tolerate. Many conductors obeyed him because he held their recording futures in his pocket. Soloists, too, revered his signature on their contracts. He was a big man in a big job and he meant people to know it.

Unfortunately for Legge, nobody had informed Sir Arthur Bliss of this fact. Perhaps composers were less susceptible to his seeming omnipotence.

One day Sir Arthur was in the studio with the Philharmonia recording some of his own music, when Legge, the producer, decided to make one of his regular forays onto the studio floor with a list of required improvements to the performance which he was confident Sir Arthur had overlooked and would accept.

Legge was full of himself. But as soon as he began his catalogue of points Sir Arthur, who had a very clear idea of Legge's place in the creative scheme of things, turned on him.

'Get back to your box, little man,' he snapped

in front of Legge's amazed orchestra. Legge slunk back to the recording booth, temporarily deflated.

♩

Paul Hindemith, apart from being a superb composer and a skilled conductor, had been in earlier years an orchestral viola player. Someone asked him why he had given up playing in an orchestra.

'Everything was fine. I was in an excellent orchestra and for many years I was its principal viola. As with everything, though, there was a problem. Almost every month we had a new conductor to take us in our regular concerts.

'The only trouble was they all wanted to do the First Symphony of Brahms. Everything used to go well until we reached the last movement. Then, when we had passed that monumental introduction, the conductor would stop the orchestra and look at the principal horn.

' "In your solo," he would say, "try to make it sound as if the sun has just come out."

'I heard every conductor we ever had say that! I heard it twenty, thirty, even, fifty times, and I grew to hate it! Even to anticipate it. I began to look forward to the day when my luck would change.

'Then, one day, I heard that Bruno Walter was going to conduct us. What do you think he'd chosen? Brahms' First Symphony, of course. But this time I knew it would be different. The rehearsal was tremendous. The horn played his part beautifully. I was really happy by the end.

'As I walked backstage I passed the open door of the maestro's room. He had his arm round the horn player's shoulders.

' "Do you know," he was saying, "when you played that big solo in the last movement, it sounded just as if the sun had come out!"

'I couldn't bear it any more – so I took to composing instead!'

In the early 1960s Sir Adrian Boult was rehearsing the London Philharmonic in the First Symphony of the English composer Humphrey Searle.

Boult was well over six feet tall and was standing on a platform some five feet above the level of the seats in the hall. The composer, who wrote in the atonal style then so fashionable, had decided to attend.

Once the rehearsal began Sir Adrian noticed that the trumpets were playing something different from his score.

'What have you got there?' he demanded.

'Concert B-flats,' they replied.

'That's not what's in the score,' he muttered, and he turned to look for the composer in the gloom of the hall.

'Composer!' he yelled.

Up came Searle, a score in his hand. As he approached he was forced to crane his head backwards to see the ramrod figure of the conductor high above.

'They've got B-flats. I've got Cs. Now, which do you want?' Sir Adrian asked.

The composer checked his score. 'Cs, Sir Adrian,' he confirmed.

'Right.' Boult turned to the trumpets. 'Change your parts to Cs.'

The rehearsal continued for a few bars until a similar situation arose with the horns.

'Composer!' shouted Boult.

Along came the composer, and the horn players' parts were changed to accommodate his intentions. But this pattern was repeated with different sections of the orchestra on too many occasions for Boult to continue seeking the composer's advice. Instead, he began to make his own alterations to the detail of Searle's symphony.

The composer listened and watched in silence until, during the last movement, he noticed something he wished to change which Boult had not picked up.

'Sir Adrian,' he called diffidently from the foot of the platform to the determined figure above him. 'Sir Adrian. There's something I'd like to mention.'

But Sir Adrian went on rehearsing, apparently oblivious of the supplicant below.

'Sir Adrian,' Searle repeated, 'Sir Adrian.'

But Boult had had enough of interruptions and alterations. He turned brusquely and snapped, 'Go away, little man. We're not playing your piece.'

THE ORCHESTRA
STRIKES BACK

At the turn of the century Hans Richter, widely considered to be the foremost German conductor of the day, came to England to conduct a London orchestra in some Beethoven symphonies.

At that time the 'deputy system' was even more widely used than it is today. Under this system any member of an orchestra, if he could get more money for another engagement, could send along a replacement for a rehearsal or even for the concert itself. Such a way of life was largely unknown on the continent.

Richter was delighted with the first rehearsal but, during the second, he noticed that some players were different. By the third rehearsal still more musicians had been replaced by newcomers.

He was about to begin the last rehearsal when he noticed that only one player, from the double-bass section, remained from the first rehearsal. Slowly he made his way through the orchestra until he came face to face with the survivor.

'I would like to thank you so much,' he began with heavy irony, 'for staying with me. Thank you.'

'That's all right,' the man replied, with a pleasant smile. 'I enjoyed it a lot. I only wish I could do the concert as well.'

♩

In his early days, Isidore Godfrey, who came to make a career conducting Gilbert and Sullivan, found himself directing an orchestra whose cello section included a lady wearing a large hat piled high with swathes of net and cloth. Its crowning glory was an exceptionally splendid feather at least a foot long.

Godfrey asked her to remove the hat, but she refused. No matter how hard he tried, he failed to shake her resolve. He attempted to ignore the monstrous hat, to pretend it wasn't there. But he couldn't. The feather always contrived to jerk slightly behind the beat, creating a continual distraction.

Eventually he could bear it no longer.

'Madam,' he snapped, 'why can't you try following my beat?'

The lady looked up from beneath the overhanging brim.

'Young man,' she declared, 'if you're not careful, I shall.'

♩

During the 1950s the Philharmonia was streets

ahead of all other British orchestras, being generally considered one of the finest in the world. But its members were all virtuosos and were not readily amenable to the sort of corporate discipline widespread among European ensembles.

It was at this time that they had foisted on them the great Herbert Von Karajan who expected the same sort of respect and humility in Britain that he enjoyed in Berlin and Vienna. Unfortunately for him, unlike their counterparts in most continental cities, London musicians, then as now, were not dependent upon one solitary orchestra for their living. They enjoyed a choice of several and, in any case, were self-employed, which further increased their capacity for outspokenness.

Among the first violins of the Philharmonia sat an ex-Spitfire pilot, Peter Gibbs. The war had been over no more than six or seven years and Germany still lay in ruins. The sight of an ex-member of the ex-master race on the rostrum demanding something only slightly less than total idolatry was not guaranteed to bring out Mr Gibbs' more conciliatory qualities.

For several sessions the orchestra tolerated what they considered to be the overbearing and unreasonable demands of the maestro. But eventually Gibbs could stand no more. Leaping to his feet, he declared in ringing tones, heavy with menace, 'I've just spent five years of my life shooting people like you out of the sky and I don't see why I should put up with this sort of thing here! Do you understand?'

The Royal Philharmonic Orchestra was rehearsing *Scheherazade*. This was not one of those magical occasions when Beecham revealed the secrets of Rimsky-Korsakov's colourful suite. The conductor was Royalton Kisch. It would be fair to say that he was less skilled in his handling of *rubato* than Sir Thomas.

The principal bassoonist of the RPO played with considerable rhythmic freedom and heightened expressiveness, which his principal conductor seemed never to have considered discouraging.

When the big bassoon solo in the 'Kalendar Prince' was reached, the player phrased it even more elastically than usual. The rest of the orchestra watched and marvelled with little grins of amusement at the conductor's predicament.

Mr Kisch was desperately trying to follow the soloist's beat but, defeated by such a display of virtuoso flexibility, was left to carve the air in frustration. He took his head from the score, stopped beating and looked up.

'Look,' he began, 'when we get to this bit tonight, perhaps I won't bother to conduct it.'

The bassoonist raised his eyes over the top of his glasses.

'Why?' he inquired guilelessly. 'Were you?'

The eminent Bavarian conductor Eugen Jochum was considered by the players of the London Symphony Orchestra to resemble pretty closely, in the shape of his head and the way in which he carried himself, Frankenstein's celebrated monster.

During a concert in the Royal Festival Hall one of his heavy gold cufflinks dropped from his shirt cuff at a climactic point in the work. It fell with a dull thud to the stage at the feet of the principal second violinist.

The violinist stared for a moment then announced (not *sotto voce*), 'The bolt's just dropped out of his bloody neck!'

The Royal Philharmonic Orchestra was on tour overseas under the charge of two different conductors. One was extremely competent but the other was not much better than an average amateur. Quite why he had been engaged for the tour was a bit of a mystery.

A particular difficulty that the musicians faced with this maestro was his choice of works, which were full of pitfalls for the best in the world, let alone a conductor of his standing.

At one early rehearsal he became entangled in a tricky bridge passage and found it impossible to steer the orchestra through the rapids to calmer waters beyond. He was offered much advice. Some he took and some he failed to understand, but the players did what players will always do in such circumstances: they strove to see that the actual performance would be as good as possible.

Eventually, after much struggle and guidance (including the principal oboe standing up and marking time for the conductor's benefit), the maestro managed to beat his way through what Sir Adrian Boult would probably have called a 'gearchange'.

Everyone smiled; the conductor looked triumphant, certain of success. But from the brass section came a quiet voice of reason. 'OK. So we're over Becher's Brook. There's still thirty fences to go!'

♩

By the mid 1970s many of Britain's regional orchestras had become a little tainted by the prevailing attitudes of trades unions. Often these orchestras owed their very existence to the sterling efforts of a handful of devoted conductors: in

Manchester there was Barbirolli, in Glasgow music's champion was Sir Alexander Gibson. He had saved the Scottish National Orchestra from extinction, going on to advance the cause of opera of the highest standard by creating, virtually on his own, Scottish Opera.

During some recording sessions with the Scottish National Orchestra it became apparent, because the recording had gone so well, that there would be a considerable amount of spare time at the end of the session.

'What shall we do with the remaining time?' Sir Alexander asked the recording manager over lunch. 'I would love to record some Delius if I could. Whatever we do could always go towards another record.'

So, when the recording of the originally scheduled music had been completed, Sir Alexander told the orchestra that the librarian was about to put out some additional music for them to record in the remaining time. There were murmurs of discontent from the players.

'We've finishd what we were supposed to record,' one said, 'so we should be allowed to go home. If we've been good enough to complete the recording early, why should we be penalised and kept here longer?'

His colleagues' support was plain to see. Sir Alexander looked puzzled.

'Look here,' he began, 'it's not easy getting recording people to come up here from London to make records. If I had been working with the

LSO or the LPO this afternoon, do you suppose they would argue about it? No, they wouldn't. They'd get on with it. Which is what we've got to do. It's the way of the world.'

More mutterings greeted this sally.

'OK,' declared the exasperated conductor, the man who had kept them in their jobs for so many years, 'let's get this straight once and for all. What do you want to be? An orchestra of international standing – or a provincial band?'

Without hesitation, up went the shout, 'Provincial band!'

The recording went ahead, but was never issued.

♩

The major orchestras hold auditions from time to time – even though they often have a shrewd idea who might be the right person for any new vacancy.

During the late Sir John Pritchard's reign as principal conductor of the London Philharmonic, an audition for violinists was held in one of the smaller side rooms of the Royal Albert Hall.

Several people had already appeared before the panel of Sir John and principal players of the orchestra, when a middle-aged man appeared, clutching a new violin case and some yellowing music.

122

'What'd you like me to play?' the violinist asked in a ripe Northern accent, as he raised his fiddle.

'Whatever you like,' replied Sir John, at which the fiddler began to play in the most amateurish way. The panel of judges sat in acute embarrassment, uncertain what to do or say. Nothing similar had ever happened to them before.

'OK?' the man enquired. 'What'd you like next?'

Sir John, a smooth man, a sophisticated man, someone well able to cope with all situations – in short a conductor – was defeated by this show of outright incompetence. What could he say? Was it a joke? Was this man trying to make some heavy point? He and his colleagues from the LPO sat in silence.

After a few moments the violinist bent down, picked up his case and said, 'Admit it, I'm no bloody good, am I?'

Sir John was forced to agree with him that, on the evidence so far . . .

'I know I'm rubbish,' the man continued. 'Can you put it in writing? Will you write to me and say I'm no damned good? You see, I'm that fed up with my wife going on to me about my playing. She keeps on saying that I'm so wonderful I should be in the ruddy London Philharmonic. If you write and say I'm rubbish perhaps she'll leave me alone.'

On another occasion Norman Foster, the ebullient American violinist, was auditioning for the London Symphony Orchestra. Auditions are never liked and have been known to bring out the worst in everyone involved.

'What are you going to play?' André Previn, the orchestra's principal conductor, wanted to know as Foster lodged his music on the stand.

'If you don't know it when you hear it, then we're both wasting our time,' he replied.

Harry Legge, for many years a fine viola player and teacher, has played in all the great orchestras and under most of the best conductors.

A few years ago he was rehearsing on the South Coast with a small London chamber orchestra, under the direction of its principal conductor who had also become its new owner.

The rehearsal went smoothly enough and tea-time approached. Harry decided on a stroll along the sea front, followed by a snack in a small café before the evening's concert.

The café he selected soon became very crowded and before very long he was forced to share his table. After a few minutes he fell into conversation with his new neighbour. They talked of this and that and of that and this, until

Harry, looking sharply at the man's face, said, 'You know, your face is vaguely familiar. I'm sure we must have met somewhere.'

'Yes,' the man replied, 'I shouldn't be surprised. I've been rehearsing you all afternoon. I'm your conductor.'

LAST WORD

Josef Krips was a devout man. He had studied under Weingartner and, when only thirty-three years old, appeared at the Salzburg Festival. He was a fine interpreter of the greatest Austrian composers, particularly Mozart and Schubert, and had survived the war by acting as a clandestine opera coach in Vienna.

He was chief conductor of the London Symphony Orchestra during the 1950s, which doubtless broadened his extra-musical horizons.

Self-governing orchestras do not exist in quite the same way outside London.

At all events, by the time he found himself directing a series of concerts in Vienna with the Philharmonia Orchestra, he thought it advisable to call a prayer meeting beforehand.

All the principals of the orchestra assembled in his office and stood in a circle. With their eyes cast down and their hands loosely clasped, the players listened to the cherubic Krips intone his hopes and expectations to the Almighty.

'By the grace of God, and if we manage to keep the oboe solo down, we shall have a successful concert.'

'Amen,' they murmured.